The Suitable Girl

I'm indebted to Dale Wallace, Pascale Petit, Ian Duhig, Vicki Feaver, Fiona Zerbst, Joanne Limburg, Helen Ivory, Gaia Holmes, Ian Parks, Roy Woolley, Jo Hemmant and, in particular, Molly McGrane.

The Suitable Girl

Michelle McGrane

Pindrop Press

Published 2010 by
Pindrop Press
Mallards
Steers Place
Hadlow
Tonbridge
TN11 0HA
www.pindroppress.com

ISBN 978-0-9567822-0-5

A catalogue record for this book is available from the British Library.

Typeset by Pindrop Press.

Printed and bound in the UK by the MPG Books Group, Bodmin and King's Lynn.

Cover image courtesy of ©iStockphoto.com/ChuckSchugPhotography

*For my mother,
and in memory of my father*

Contents

The Art of Awakening, 10
Lunar Postcards, 11
    I   Moondust
    II Hadley Rille
    III Space Gourmet
    IV Counting Clusters
Bonsai, 15
4.00 am, 16
The Bridal Robe, 17
The Bee Man, 18
Wearing Silence, 19
January Triptych, 20
    I   Father
    II Grief
    III Grace
The Blue Door Opens, 23
The Escape Artist, 24
Bertha Mason Speaks, 25
Augusta Fabergé, 26
Ipatiev House, July 1918, 27
The Recalcitrant Muse, 28
Black Sparrowhawk, 29
Thirteen Ways with Figs, 30
The Court Confectioner, 33
Skin Offerings, 34
If You are Lucky, 36
Casa Magni, July 1822, 38

The Remise of Marie Antoinette, aged 14, 39
Princess de Lamballe, 40
The Discovery Shed, 41
Madame Bovary's Final Visit, 42
Frangipani Night, 43
She Walks on Water, 44
The Mary Celeste, 45
Black Oak's Daughter, 46
Half the Secret, 47
'Terra Marique Potens', 48
Gallows Bird, 49
Along the Corpse Road, 50

9

The Art of Awakening

Pale-faced and resolute,
the four women wait
to step out of their ink drawing
and walk into the world.

Any second, you will see
a blue vein pulse, an eyelid flutter,
the stretching of a stiff neck.

Now,
the quickening breath,
the rapid heartbeat
as blood blossoms through the body.

How one woman
might turn to another
and with untried muscles, smile
before straightening her shoulders
and moving forward, slowly,
to enter the strange, mercurial light.

Lunar Postcards

I. Moondust

Two hours ago, we docked
at Crater Plaskett's northern rim.
Plumes of spent gunpowder
eructed from the landing strip,
spinning into galaxies and starfields.
It clings to our helmet visors,
sifts into our spacesuits,
fine, jagged particles
infiltrating hinges and joints,
scratching equipment,
shrouding instrument dials
with an electrostatic film.

II.   Hadley Rille

I am writing from a lava tube
at Hadley Rille, near the Sea of Rains.
We spent the day gathering
silica-rich soil, shattered rocks,
glassy, fist-sized specimens
sampled from the basalt crust.
The Lunar Roving Vehicle
has exceeded all expectations.
Jack and his crew will be pleased.
I look forward to your news.

III.   Space Gourmet

We season freeze-dried macaroni
with liquid salt and pepper.
Water is distilled, recycled
from our breath and sweat.
After a week of granola bars,
nuts and bitter orange juice,
the commander's arm
begins to look tasty.

IV. Counting Clusters

At night,
the lunar module
ticks and hums.
I shift restlessly
in my stellar nursery,
trace the constellations
of your freckles,
striving to sail
these light years
home to you.

Bonsai

Finally, I was free to disappear
the day my husband
brought the young brush cherry home.
He settled her on the stand
between the firethorn and crab apple,
then mended the mossy wooden fence
along the property boundaries.

I knew she was different
by her tapering trunk,
glossy, red foliage,
heavy lower branches
and well-distributed roots.
Oh, she was ornamental enough.
He'd always had an eye for potential.

Through the bedroom curtain,
I watched her peel twenty years off his age.
He couldn't keep the smile from his face,
spent the evening kneeling in the garden,
singing green heart notes
to her sprouting, elliptic leaves.

No more fingering,
pinching, pruning, bleeding,
every branch and twig wired,
brown and flexible, bent to the shape
of his fingers and thumbs.

Waking in the early morning, I left him
wrapped in dreams of sweet, red flesh,
the sunlight glinting off my node scars.

4.00 am

The young mother rises in silence
from the rough pinewood pallet on the floor.
Curled together under their musty, grey blanket,
the children breathe easily and do not stir.
She, a stooped shadow groping in darkness,
draws the darned widow's dress
over her bony shoulders and chest –
inhaling her body's odour –
covering the grape-sized sores on her legs.
All around she hears the rustling presence
of the watchful, impassive dead.
She rubs her tired eyes and coughs. Sharply.
The small mud hut is sour, airless.
Her captured lungs are intricate knots.
She leaves two, sticky-soft bananas
on a scratched plastic plate for when they awake.
In the chill of morning, she latches the door
and sets out north, along a narrow dirt road,
twelve kilometres over precarious farmland,
to the crammed, weekly government clinic.
From down here, in the crowded bone valley,
Saturn rides high in the sky.
The air is swollen with damp earth and lantana.
She walks slowly, softly humming a hymn
while the cold wind flutters the ends
of her gaily-patterned headscarf.

The Bridal Robe

Tonight the isthmus city
floats on waves of apple blossoms,
and while temple prostitutes dream
of husbands, I wait at the window,

coaxed to life in Medea's hands,
soft folds draped on a willow stand,
lit by the Aegean moon.

Tomorrow is the wedding feast
and I, sheathing her skin in fine pleats,
scalloped hem grazing sandalled feet,
the talk of Corinth.

The Bee Man

Just before the old man died,
his honey bees deserted their hives
among the lacy, white almond trees,

swarming across the cottage roof,
the electric charge heard for miles.

A single bee flew through the window,
a winged emissary navigating shutter
and cream curtain, to hover

above the keeper's cheek, then alight,
anointing him with a golden streak –

protection in the underworld.

Wearing Silence

On the day of your funeral
the air hums; everything is green.

I sprawl on the lawn in the sun,
wearing silence

         and watch
a small, white butterfly flutter by

through the vault of old oaks
and up over the garden wall.

January Triptych

I Father

The coffin is unvarnished pine
with six rope handles,
tawny resin beading a seam.

The viewing room is empty.
You are gone,
striding out across the veld
heeled by our childhood hounds.

Someone
should have warned the undertaker
you would never agree
to lie in this box.

II Grief

It arrives in the mail
with a licence renewal,

wears the thin, grey socks
never returned.

It curls up, settles in
where I least expect –

a note slipped between pages,
a bald head in a supermarket queue.

III Grace

The day she brings your ashes home,
my mother cradles the box to her breast
before placing it in a cool cupboard.

In a kitchen, miles away,
I unsheathe long-stemmed roses –

removing thorns and leaves,
trimming stalks –

the creamy-green guard petals
beginning to open.

Rising, then receding,
her voice wavers through the telephone –

and, here, in my fingers,
the cellophane label, 'Esperance'

The Blue Door Opens

Twirling her parasol,
the cow lows from Vitebsk roofs,
candles circle the covered corpse.

In shadows
he maps a herring,
a wheatfield, a yellow boat.

He hears folksongs
along the swift Dvina;
sees the sickle moon
outside a slanted window.

Night blooms coral peonies,
bamboo fans and mandolins;
rows of soldiers and menorahs
wend through cemetery gates.

Crumpled sheets rise and fall
across a lovers' airless room:
an outstretched arm, a pale thigh,
silk petticoats whisper in a chair.

He somersaults
above the bride,
the clock, the ferris wheel.
He soars
beyond the singing goat
nesting in an autumn tree.

The Escape Artist

In our three-month acquaintance, Faolán was known throughout circus rings as the Lord of the Fleas. Faolán means 'little wolf'. He was a hairy wee beastie. Agile, a born entertainer and ambitious to boot. Nothing short of global domination would satisfy the Lilliputian star. From tenth generation Saratov Circus stock on his paternal side, his mother was Muirne Mac Nessa, the Irish siphonaptera racing champion. People journeyed from as far as Argentina and the Macau Peninsula to marvel at his mesmerising chariot act, dazzling tightrope performance, virtuoso cannon routine and death-defying fire dance.

There was no one to blame but myself when he ran off with the ringmaster's silver weimaraner. I should have suspected something was amiss. He stopped feeding when the laughing, long-haired bitch sashayed past his trailer, refused to turn cartwheels as I greeted him from behind the magnifying glass. Now, I'm training aerial silk artistes. Of course, it's not the same. My heart's no longer in the hyperbole. Does he miss the good times, the spotlight, the smell of roast chestnuts and candyfloss, the cheering crowds? I sleep with his gold-trimmed tophat and tails, his diminutive whip, in a snuffbox beside my bed.

Bertha Mason Speaks

Now that you've heard Jane's side of the story, what I wish to tell you is this:

that once I had hoped to be happy with my cold, dour-faced husband somewhere in the periphery; that, in retrospect, the day he came for me was the day my island spirit deserted me; that the exile from my ramshackle green home caused something within me to tear adrift;

that I dreamed of sticky-sweet mango strings caught between my teeth, awaking with a salty mosaic tattooed on my lips; that I basked naked in the arms of a calypso moon with seashells gleaming in my untamed mane; that all of the bonnets and baubles in Christendom could not compare to the sunshine of Spanish Town;

that I floated on a celestial conflagration of saffron frangipani only to plummet, petrified, into a voodoo tomb; that within these stone walls time became obsolete: no market days, no festivals, no seasonal ebb and flow; that mocking echoes dogged this stifling boudoir and rattled within my bones;

that while I stalked the corridors of the haunted mausoleum, cinders and sparks showered their benedictions upon me; that I invoked the shapes of incandescent fever-trees, both eclipsed candle and hungry flame; that I sang, blood-red, the island's setting sun, despite my dislocated tongue.

Augusta Fabergé

Following Bolshaya Morskaya's stone sweep,
I hurry his meal, sautéed carp *pirozhki*,
a shoal of small pies caught in my hands,
their heat rising through the unbleached linen.

At his weathered workbench, craftsmen flock
exclaiming over the Rosebud Egg,
an Imperial Easter gift from the new Tsar
to his blue-blooded beloved, Alexandra.

Within the guillochéd, strawberry-red carapace,
hinged, yellow enamel petals unfurl
revealing a cabochon ruby pendant and crown
never meant for a plain cabinetmaker's daughter.

Ipatiev House, July 1918

Some days, we're allowed a quiet hour
in the garden. The girls and I sit on the grass,
pearls and diamonds stitched into our corsets.
Alyoshenka dozes, confined to his wheelchair
since the sledding accident on the stairs at Tobolsk.
Yevgeny says he will never walk again.

Beneath palsied poplars, birches and limes,
Nicholas paces the pine palisade, split planks
imprisoning the Voznessenski Street property.
My husband has aged, trim beard streaked grey.
He never wanted to be Tsar.

I search the sky for sun-grazing comets,
the pattern and movement of cumulus clouds,
some divine sign from Our Friend, Rasputin.
A murder of crows recedes on dark wings,
cleaving light, fleeing our fated daguerreotype,
a strangled screech taking seed in my throat.

The Recalcitrant Muse

Sunlight blisters through moth-eaten curtains.
In her mildewed apartment high above the city,
the Muse stumbles out of bed, stubs her toe
in the kitchen as she fumbles for a cigarette,
reheats last night's coffee and loneliness,
gulps it down dark, bitter, thick with grounds
that refuse to dissolve her tongue's furred lining.

She is late for the morning's first appointment
with a middle-aged divorcée at 52 East Avenue.
It's not all it's cracked up to be, this muse business.
She's tired of being aloof, untouchable.
Give me strong hands, warm flesh, a hairy chest,
a plunging prick, fucking on the formica table.
She could use a drink. A few hours' sleep.
Immortality doesn't pay the bills.

Black Sparrowhawk

Swooping through the door after a laughing dove,
you didn't anticipate the rufous streak –
your prey escaping in the afternoon heat –

as you flew deeper into the house, past the teak kist,
along the passage, alighting in the bathroom,
your talons scraping against the tiles.

Afraid you would injure yourself, I cracked the door,
dialled Raptor Rescue in Cato Ridge, sat
cross-legged outside, listening for calls of distress.

"A juvenile female", the ornithologist said,
pointing to your brown plumage, then releasing you
between the Johannesburg gold and the strelitzia,

where you rose to perch in eucalyptus shade,
a few yards from the padlocked shed –
red-eyed, wary, almost hidden.

Thirteen Ways with Figs

1.

Silence the village gossip with nutty figs
rolled in crushed peppercorns.
Layer the fiery fruit in a jar between bay leaves.
Store in a dark place for three days.
Leave your offering on her doorstep.

2.

Sweeten your mother-in-law,
a small, crepey woman in a black dress
smelling of mothballs,
with stuffed quails roasted in thick balsamic sauce,
followed by ricotta-rose cheesecake and marzipan-filled figs.
Spill velvet-pink petals over her plate.

3.

Soothe inflamed ulcers and lesions
with a steamed fig, slippery elm, flaxseed poultice.
Wrap around the weeping skin in a muslin cloth.

4.

Pick a ribbed fig from the tree at twilight.
Split the dark cocoon in two.
Rub the wart with amber pulp and seeds.
Tie the halves together again.
Bury them in the flinty earth
under the waning moon.

5.

Cure fatigue, insomnia or nightmares
by boiling milk poured in a pail
with sun-baked figs and turmeric.
Add lavender honey to taste. Drink slowly.

6.
Bind three, white Cilento figs
with a crimson ribbon for dreams of love.
Place the fruit under your pillow.
In the morning,
loop the ribbon around your waist.
If your heart is in your mouth,
sear it, eat it with figs.

7.

Beguile your partner with fig-leaf *absolute*
dabbed along the curve of your neck.
Wear almond blossoms in your hair.
Dance on a terrace with a view of the harbour,
to the flashing grin of an accordionist
who smells of sulphur and plays like the devil.
Clap your hands. This is no time to tiptoe.

8.

On a balmy midsummer evening, wrap up your *al fresco* meal
at the warped wooden table under the plane tree
with grilled figs, spoonfuls of soft mascarpone
drizzled with orange blossom and rose water.
Smell the mimosa.
Don't wipe the sugary smudge from your chin.
Carry the sated silence to bed.

9.

Arouse your lover with plump, purple figs in a cool bowl of water.
Break the thin, moist skin with your fingers.
Close your eyes. Listen to your breathing.

10.

On a windy day welcome your new neighbours across the pasture.
Make them feel at home with *capocollo*,
a sausage of figs, almonds, pistachios and cinnamon.
Fold in leaves
left in a basket on the porch. Follow the dung
trail home, a wasp
hovering at your shoulder.

11.

In autumn, line your pantry shelves with jars of fig jam
scented with cardamom pods. Seal in the sunshine
with smooth wax discs and screw-top lids.

12.

Feed a hungry family
with slow-cooked pork loin and Adriatic fig stuffing.
Serve with golden polenta. Garnish with watercress.
Open bottles of the full-bodied local wine.
Taste the olive-wood smoke,
the measure of November's indulgences.

13.

When the sky pops and hisses with stars,
celebrate the year's trailing tail.
Prepare fig fillets stuffed with amaretti *biscotti*
and smoky, chocolate slivers.
Serve with steaming espressos before midnight.
Va bene.

The Court Confectioner

Forty years I've toiled in this kitchen,
seen queens rise and fall, shenanigans
I wouldn't confide to a soul
for fear of the hangman's noose.
Guard your tongue, I've always said,
and keep your eyes on the marchpane.

God knows, I've had my fill of feasts,
tempting fickle palates with sweetmeats,
the last word in subtyltes and conceyts
as crafted by masters in Paris and Naples:
trompe l'oeil dainties, gilded sugar-plums,
barberry doucets and spun-sugar swans.

Now I've a mind to retire up north,
keep company with my sister-in-law,
open a pie stall with a bright awning,
serve honest fare, no tricks or frills.
Market days I'll reap reward enough
warming cottars' bellies.

Skin Offerings

You surprised,
no – *terrified* –
        me,
when I visited the hospital.

You'd committed yourself –
after all –

I'd thought you wanted
to get well.

Silence, anger, tears,
I was prepared for any eventuality,
except
sharp-edged, smiling resolve.

Your body, turned cannibal,
is devouring itself.

I wonder, elf-girl,
where you find
the strength, determination
to starve yourself
when there is
        so little
of you left.

With shadowy satisfaction
you tell me
you are still
        refusing to eat;
the nurses have threatened to
put you in lock-up.

You exhibit mutilation marks:
angry, red welts, fluid-filled blisters,

sin offerings, skin offerings.

On bony wrists, on
        your neck, *for god's sake!*
you've burnt patterns
        on your skin
with a lighter.

Your religion: concave stomach,
protruding bones;
offered prayers, laxatives and
valium.

If You are Lucky

If you are lucky
you will carry one night with you
for the rest of your life,
a night like no other.
You won't see it coming.

Forget the day, the year.
It will arrive uninvoked,
an astrological anomaly.

You will remember
how every cell in your body
knew him, this stranger,

how you held your breath,
the way you searched his face.
This is how such evenings begin.

And you will be real in your skin,
bone and sinew; the way you always thought
you could be. Effortlessly.
This is how you will fit together.

His parted lips between your thighs,
your half-lit nipples darkening,
the hot-breathed arrival of desire,
the frenzied coupling
as you opened soundlessly
and the world flooded into you.

In the morning, maybe,
soon after sunrise
you will walk barefoot above a waterfall in the forest,
light-headed with the smell of sex,
laughing in your *déshabillée*.

You will carry
the music of this memory with you;
and from time to time,
in the small, withered hours,
your body will sing its remembering.

Casa Magni, July 1822

Five days seemed like twelve
without word from Shelley.

I sat on the terrace,
his telescope in my lap,

waited for *Ariel*,
a flash of white sail –

Byron's *Don Juan*
excised by the *velaio*.

I tried to remember
if I'd ever liked San Terenzo:

the converted boathouse,
shabby fishing hamlet,

squabbling servants,
our friends, the three children,

and the bay of La Spezia,
blue and inscrutable.

The Remise of Marie Antoinette, aged 14

Far from Vienna, a curlew's liquid trill ripples the air. Willows bracing the muddy bank dip and trail fronds through the Rhine's swift currents. On the Île des Épis, a pavilion. Organza rustles, Sèvres porcelain tinkles on a silver salver. The smell of *chocolat chaud* pervades the tapestried salon. (To the right, Jason grieves over his children's corpses, to the left, Medea flees in her dragon-drawn chariot.)

They strip me, leaving Austria crumpled at my feet, lacing the whalebone corset so tightly I can scarcely breathe. Circling and circling, the coiffured courtiers slyly eye my flushed cheeks, newly formed breasts and hips, tittering *pianissimo* behind lacquered fans. The Duchesse de Picquigny twitters in her sing-song voice, a bright-eyed parakeet. The beaked Comtesse de Noailles buttons me into cloth-of-gold, fingers needling, lips carved in a permanent moue.

Stiff curls piled on her head, Madame la Dauphine enters the country of loneliness in silk stockings and satin mules while I, slipping from beneath her powdered skin, edge out of the frame, steal through taffeta curtains barefoot, past gilded caryatids, silver-wigged footmen in fleur-de-lys. Diving into the green river, a purseful of livres seamed in my chemise, I strike out for wild bird calls, ragged long grass, wet earth.

Princesse de Lamballe

He skewers my matted, blonde head on a pike,
shows me the city's less-fêted sights:
growling alleys and ravenous back streets
guttered with urine, nightsoil and vermin;
toothless, frayed women queuing for bread,
each coarse, weevilled loaf fourteen copper *sous*;
the Hôpital des Quinze-Vingt's shuffling inmates
tapping for alms amid the stalls of Les Halles;
Saint-Marcel tanneries' frame-stretched hides
kneaded supple with beef greaves and brains;
the Seine choked with debris and tangled milfoil,
a carcass sliding into the Pont Neuf's shadows.

The Queen's playing *tric-trac* in the tower,
twenty guards flanking the Temple's iron portal.
She's raised the stakes, the bone dice clattering
across the pearwood and ebony board.
The scrofulous *sans-culotte* belting *Ça Ira*
braces my face to the crosshatched casing,
my fractured cheek arch, bloodied tongue,
smashed teeth, splintered jaw.
Remember Petit Trianon, ma chérie,
the dovecote and mill, cherry orchard and lake.
Remember the hyacinths we planted last autumn,
how we split our sides milking the goats.

The Discovery Shed

A dissection room annexed to the Physics School,
considered unfit for death; we make it our own
despite the *leaking roof,* the *bituminous floor.*

Closeted here, we study radium and polonium
in compounds separated from uranium ore,
witnessed only by the tables and stove,

and pages scrawled with calculations,
chemical processes, sublimation procedures,
isolation and crystallization techniques.

For lunch, a baguette, a wedge of Gruyère,
prepared on the bench beside Pierre's electrometer,
crumbs swept up hastily to discourage rats.

We dream of a dry, ventilated laboratory,
a chimney, a cistern, several portable furnaces,
a storeroom to house the hazardous substances.

Some nights, while Irène sleeps, we retrace
our steps along rue Lhomond, peer into the shed
at our phosphorescent test tubes.

Madame Bovary's Final Visit

Not difficult after all then,
slipping past the apothecary's apprentice,
the counter, scale, mortar and pestle,
through the laboratory's glass door
to seize the *Capharnaum* key.

Upstairs, in his sanctuary,
phials and pharmacopoeias,
pill dispensers, distilled elixirs,
tinctures and pewter leech carriers
jostled on mahogany shelves.

Grasping the octagonal jar,
I lifted a powder-filled fist
to my lips, my throat constricted
with deceit and its answer.
Arsenic streaked my chin.

In the pillared market square,
laughter swilled from The Golden Lion,
a conspiracy of gossip and innuendoes,
those provincial diversions,
splashed into the night.

Frangipani Night

We barter for a red and green lobster
with Radama, the fisherman's son.
It's alive. Barely half a kilogram.
Antennae waving, abdomen curling and uncurling,
the small, shelled body fits into the palm of your hand.

We help push the *pirogue* off the sand,
wavelets lapping against the *arofy* bow and hull,
before climbing the rusted ladder
to the shabby cottage perched above the bay.

You drop the crustacean into a pot of boiling water;
it scrabbles, trapped air expands
escaping the shell with a piercing whistle.
My stomach lurches and pitches.

Outside, on the ivy-clad verandah
a sphinx moth sizzles in the flickering flame.
Fruit bats swoop and glide
between the bozy baobab's branches.

We sit in silence gazing into darkness,
a coconut shell of shredded seafood
and a bottle of cheap Malagasy rum between us.
The frangipani blossoms strewn on the table
have started to wither, brown at the edges,
spotting a trail of milky sap
across our makeshift tablecloth.

She Walks on Water

The air is heavy with salt spray and kelp.
The seagull's tongue is dumb.
Dark hair hides the face
of the madonna on the beach.

Hands like silver starfish
lift a long skirt, reveal pale knees;
a cerulean scarf flutters in the breeze.

She turns away from
the promenade's ice-cream smiles
and waving kites,
shrugs off the dirty-weekend hotel
moored in the harbour's embrace.

Her spirit becomes a sail.
Her eyes are the horizon.
Her bare, white limbs shine
with phosphorescence.
The stars lean over to plant kisses
on her forehead.

In the morning haze,
wisps of fog drifting in with the waves,
she walks on water.

A blue strand washes up on the sand
among splintered timbers, plastic wrappings,
sodden cigarette butts.
Perched on a guano-stained mast,
the seagull keeps her secret.

The Mary Celeste

Plotted pencil points
on unfurled navigation charts,
the baby girl's pink pinafore
capering on the line,

a rosewood harmonium
with handwritten sheet music,
an unstoppered bottle
of Bell Tongue Syrup,

Richardson's smudged letter
to his wife, a titian curl
nestled in a locket, and always
something else that eludes me –

Black Oak's Daughter

Beneath Oileán Chliara's cliffs
I rowed my rawhide curragh north
to Calliaghcrom Rock and back
before my twelfth summer.

Casting off my linen kirtle
for my brother's frayed britches,
I clambered up windswept ledges
plundering kittiwakes' nests.

While Eibhlín, my cousin,
was instructed in embroidery,
I taught myself to fence and feint,
a sword balanced in each hand.

Thirteen years old the day
my da's fleet sailed for Spain,
I cut my long, red braids
and stowed away on board.

Half the Secret

You could never have accused me of being pretty.
I was what they called handsome
like a favoured brood mare or wolfhound bitch.

Renowned, I could outrun every girl on the island
and most of the boys. I could swim like the wild salmon
and shoot a birch knot at thirty paces.

I could clad a byre-house with wattle and daub
and midwife a milch cow. I could till and tend herb-beds
and haul turf from the hillsides.

Only once did I long for golden hair, when
Cuán Ó Ruadháin danced with Mairéad Ó Riain
on the eve of the Midsummer Fair.

'Terra Marique Potens'

So, there we were, me and the wee 'un at my breast, nestled in my sheepskin coat, cradled by the pitch and roll, when a fearsome din broke out on deck. While Tiobóid slept the sleep of newborns, Cap'n Ó Domhnaill burst into the cabin urging me to rally the crew. Sticky with birthing, milk and sweat, cursing the eejits who wouldn't grant a woman rest after labour, I sallied above with my musketoon, legs shaking as if I'd been keelhauled from Inishlaghan to Carrigeenglass North. Through flags of smoke, a square-rigged galley, its blackjack flapping as corsairs swarmed aboard. Snugging the stock into my shoulder, I picked out a flinty crag of a man bawling like the divil hisself and assailing my lads with a boarding axe. Aiming the flared muzzle, I cocked the hammer, squeezed the trigger. When he hit the boards, mouth agape, the remaining Berbers scarpered like bilge rats. I succoured the babe wrawling for teat and ordered all hands to bear up for port.

Gallows Bird

St George's Channel
through the Dover Strait,
I sailed up the Thames
towards Greenwich.

I'd heard talk
they hanged rovers,
dangled them in cages
at Wapping Stairs.

When the prow nosed
around Blackwall Point,
I saw myself,

bones picked clean,
starlings nesting
in my ribcage.

Along the Corpse Road

We carried our dead west, their calloused soles facing away from home. As the crow flies to St Bridget's Abbey, we trudged through marsh and hungry grass, resting where the coffin stone crouched and Moyle Mac Nally chiselled his name the long winter my grandsire was buried. Days when the sou'wester swept off the Atlantic, set the blackthorn branches rattling and our teeth on edge, the men passed around poitín brewed in Sleamhnan Mac Gabhnan's still, which lit a fire in our bellies and turned our thoughts from death for a while. Sure, it was never far away and we shouldered its weight as the rain seeped down our necks, the smell of wet wool rose from our cloaks and our brogues slipped along the sunken path once more. Come the end, we would all return to the church between Knocknaveen and Croaghmore where three centuries of liturgies suffused the nave with incense and tricks of the light conjured the cochineal dragons on the chancel's ceiling to life.

Notes

The Bridal Robe
Spurned by Jason in favour of Glauce, the daughter of King Creon of Corinth, Medea sends the young princess the gift of a beautiful, enchanted bridal gown. As Glauce dresses in the poisoned robe on her wedding day, she bursts into flames and burns to death.

Augusta Fabergé
guilloché: an engraving technique in which an intricate motif is etched into metal before its surface is covered with translucent enamel.

The Court Confectioner
marchpane: marzipan

Casi Magni, July 1822
velaio: sailmaker

Ipatiev House, July 1918
In April 1918, Tsar Nicholas II, Tsarina Alexandra, their five children and four retainers were confined to Ipatiev House in Yekaterinburg. On 17 July 1918, the Romanov family and their servants were murdered by Bolsheviks in the house's basement and their corpses buried in an unmarked grave outside the Siberian town.

The Remise of Marie Antoinette, aged 14
remise: handover

Frangipani Night
pirogue: a canoe made from a hollowed tree trunk
arofy: hardwood from which pirogues are carved

'Terra Marique Potens'
Terra Marique Potens: powerful by land and sea

Acknowledgements

Many thanks to the editors of the following publications in which some of these poems first appeared: *Canopic Jar, Magma, Horizon Review, Incwadi, New Coin, ouroboros review, Showcase* (at www.laurahird.com) and *Worldscapes: A Collection of Verse.*